BEYONCÉ

BY JILL SHERMAN

AMICUS LEARNING

Inspire is published by
Amicus Learning, an imprint of Amicus
P.O. Box 227
Mankato, MN 56002
www.amicuspublishing.us

Editor: Ana Brauer
Series Designer: Kathleen Petelinsek
Book Designer and Photo Researcher: Emily Dietz

Library of Congress Cataloging-in-Publication Data
Names: Sherman, Jill, author.
Title: Beyoncé / by Jill Sherman.
Description: Mankato, MN : Amicus Learning, 2025. | Series: Inspire | Includes bibliographical references and index. | Audience: Ages 5–9 | Audience: Grades 2–3 | Summary: "Learn about global superstar Beyoncé and her accomplishments as a musician in this biography packed with photos and fact-filled text suitable for young readers. Includes a table of contents, glossary, further resources, and index" — Provided by publisher.
Identifiers: LCCN 2024012073 (print) | LCCN 2024012074 (ebook) | ISBN 9798892001014 (library binding) | ISBN 9798892001595 (paperback) | ISBN 9798892002172 (ebook)
Subjects: LCSH: Beyoncé, 1981—Juvenile literature. | Singers—United States—Biography—Juvenile literature.
Classification: LCC ML3930.K66 S54 2025 (print) | LCC ML3930.K66 (ebook) | DDC 782.42164092 [B]—dc23/eng/20240315
LC record available at https://lccn.loc.gov/2024012073
LC ebook record available at https://lccn.loc.gov/2024012074

Photo Credits: Alamy Stock Photo/Brittany Smith, 8–9; AP Photo/Chris Pizzello, cover; Getty Images/BEN STANSALL, 7, Houston Chronicle Hearst Newspapers, 10, Jeff Kravitz, 19, Kevin Mazur, 4, 14, 18, 20, 21, Kristian Dowling, 17, Michael Caulfield Archive, 13; Shutterstock/Roman Sigaev, 12

Table of Contents

Beyoncé fans are called the BeyHive.

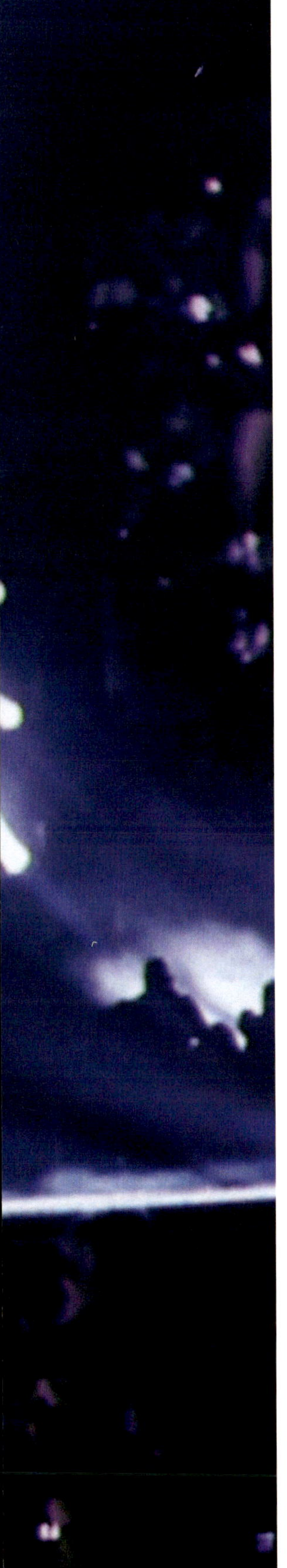

Queen Bey

Beyoncé is one of the biggest music stars today. When she takes the stage, it is clear she is in charge. Fans love how her music makes them feel strong and powerful. Beyoncé's groundbreaking music career has earned her the nickname Queen Bey.

What's in a Name?

Do you know anyone else with the name Beyoncé? Likely not. Her name came from her mom's **maiden name**. Her full name is Beyoncé Giselle Knowles. She's so famous, most people just call her Beyoncé.

Beyoncé (right) with her mom in 2012.

Beyoncé (far left) got her start with a band she started with her friends.

Search for Stardom

Beyoncé has a great voice. When she was young, she joined a singing group called Girls Tyme. In 1993, they performed on the TV show *Star Search*. They didn't win. So Beyoncé worked even harder.

Destiny's Child in 1997. Left to right: LaTavia Roberson, LeToya Luckett, Kelly Rowland, Beyoncé Knowles.

Destined for Fame

The group didn't give up. They changed their name to Destiny's Child. In 1997, they got a record deal. Their songs soon became smash hits. Destiny's Child became one of the most popular female **R&B** groups.

CHILDHOOD FRIENDS

Beyoncé grew up with the original members of Destiny's Child.

Going Solo

In 2003, Beyoncé took a risk. She made a solo album. Her voice was front and center. There was no denying it. Beyoncé was a true R&B **diva**. She recorded "Crazy in Love" with rapper Jay-Z. It was the first **single** on her album. In 2008, they got married.

NOT THE END

Beyoncé returned to Destiny's Child in 2004. They made one more album together.

Beyoncé sang at the 2003 Radio Music Awards.

Beyoncé did the famous "Single Ladies" dance at the 2013 Super Bowl halftime show.

Going Viral

Beyoncé quickly rose to fame. Her music video for "Single Ladies" went **viral** online. Justin Timberlake, Joe Jonas, and even President Obama copied the **iconic** dance moves. The song hit the top of the music **charts**.

Making Her Mark

Beyoncé makes the most of her stage time. She sang at the Video Music Awards (VMAs) in 2011. At the end of the song, she threw open her jacket. She was pregnant! Then, she performed at the 2016 Super Bowl. Beyoncé released a new song the day before. "Formation" was her song against racism.

In 2011, Beyoncé announced that she was pregnant after performing her song "Love On Top."

In 2018, Beyoncé and Jay-Z went on tour together.

Musical Family

Beyoncé's sister, Solange, has her own music career. In 2018, Beyoncé and her husband Jay-Z made an album together. They called themselves The Carters. Jay-Z's real name is Shawn Corey Carter.

Beyoncé (left) dances with Solange at a music festival in 2014.

Renaissance

Beyoncé's concerts are great fun! In 2023, Beyoncé started her **Renaissance** World Tour. She wore eye-popping costumes. Fans wore wild outfits, too! In 2024, Beyoncé released her first country album. It even won Album of the Year!

RECORD HOLDER

As of 2024, Beyoncé and Jay-Z are tied as the most nominated musicians in Grammy history.

Beyoncé sang songs from her album *Renaissance* during her 2023 tour.

SUPER STATS

BEYONCÉ KNOWLES-CARTER

Birthday: September 4, 1981

Hometown: Houston, Texas

Children: 3

AWARDS THROUGH 2024

Grammys: 35

Billboard Music Awards: 28

MTV Video Music Awards: 30

ALBUMS

Dangerously in Love (2003)

B'day (2006)

I Am...Sasha Fierce (2008)

4 (2011)

Beyoncé (2013)

Lemonade (2016)

The Lion King: The Gift (2019)

Renaissance (2022)

Cowboy Carter (2024)

THE CARTERS ALBUMS

Everything Is Love (2018)

GLOSSARY

chart A ranking of the most popular music.

diva A glamorous and successful female performer with a strong personality.

iconic Something that is widely known or easily recognized.

maiden name A person's last name before marriage.

R&B Rhythm and blues, a type of music.

renaissance A period of great artistic activity.

single A song usually released before the album.

viral Quickly and widely spread through social media.

READ MORE

Isdahl, Nansubuga Nagadya. **Beyoncé.** New York: Abrams Books for Young Readers. 2021.

Kawa, Katie. **Beyoncé: Making a Difference through Music.** KidHaven Publishing, 2022.

Moss, Caroline. **Work It, Girl: Beyoncé Knowles: Rule the Music Scene like Queen.** Quarto Publishing Group UK, 2021.

ON THE WEB

All Music
https://www.allmusic.com/artist/beyonc%C3%A9-mn0000761179

Official Website of Beyoncé
https://www.beyonce.com/

INDEX

About the Author

Jill Sherman writes books about pop stars, baby animals, and robots. She loves that writing allows her to research and learn about new topics. In addition to writing books, Jill sews her own clothes, creates crossword puzzles, and codes in JavaScript.

She listened to all of Beyoncé's music while writing this book.